KU-678-714

TELL ME ABOUT
WRITERS AND ILLUSTRATORS

DICK
KING-SMITH

written by
Chris Powling

Evans

Evans Brothers Limited

These days, Dick King-Smith is famous. All over the world children read his books. They're about bossy parrots, and hens that divebomb foxes, and hedgehogs who don't know their kerb drill...

Even grown-ups loved the movie "Babe". This was based on Dick's story "The Sheep Pig".

'I became an author quite late in life,' Dick says, 'after I'd failed at a lot of other things first!'

Here's the true story of his life so far.

Dick King-Smith... the farmer who became a writer.

5

Dick King-Smith lives in the Somerset countryside in a house that's more than three hundred and fifty years old. It's only three and a half miles from where he was born. Dick's father ran a family business making paper.

Dick and his wife Myrle in their garden.

Dick was a keen reader. He loved animal stories, especially. He also read the 'William' books by Richmal Crompton.

With his younger brother, Tony, he had a very happy childhood. 'There wasn't much traffic at that time,' he says, 'so I was able to roam the countryside on my bike.'

Dick, aged four, with his grandfather, aged 102, his grandmother and his mother

Dick and his bike

His schooldays were happy, too. At Marlborough, the famous public school, he studied Latin and Greek. 'I was reasonably intelligent... and reasonably lazy. But what I really wanted to do was live on a farm.'

Luckily, so did the girl he wanted to marry.

Dick as a teenager

Susie, Dick's favourite dog

Dick and Myrle first met when they were only 13. Their families were close friends. 'I was annoyed with her at first because she could throw stones further than I could. She was better at breeding budgies, too. This was one of our hobbies.'

Their wedding had to wait, though.

So did Dick's career as a farmer.

Dick and Myrle in their war-time uniforms

In 1939, England went to war with Germany. So Myrle joined the Royal Air Force to help spot enemy planes and Dick volunteered for the Army. He was sent to Italy as a Guards Officer. There he fought at the Salerno landings. Just south of Florence he was badly wounded. Eventually, he had to return home.

Dick wearing battle dress in Italy in 1943

After the war came a stroke of luck. 'My father's firm bought a farm. They asked me to manage it. It didn't need to make money. The milk, eggs and bacon all went to the works-canteen.'

Dick and Myrle married during the war on the 6th of February 1943.

For fourteen years, everything was fine. Dick and Myrle had two daughters, Juliet and Lizzie, and a son, Giles. At this time Dick began to write poems, just for fun. Some of them were printed in magazines like 'Punch' and 'The Field' and 'Good Housekeeping'.

Dick's children are now grown-ups. Dick also has 11 grandchildren and 1 great-grandchild.

He had an idea for a story, too. While he was milking, or looking after his pigs, Dick thought about the foxes who kept attacking his hens. Poor hens! Was there any way they could fight back?

But that's where the hen story stayed - in Dick's head. For, suddenly, his luck disappeared. The family firm had to close. So did Dick's farm. He tried another as a tenant farmer. This closed, too. 'I wasn't any good at the money-making side of farming,' he says.

As a farmer, Dick was especially fond of pigs.

Dick was a teacher at Farmborough Primary School.

Now he had to find a different job. He tried selling fire-fighting suits. He tried working in a shoe factory, then he went to college to train as a teacher in a primary school.

Teaching was just right for him... almost. He liked the children a lot. He loved the reading and writing, too. What he hated was the number work.

Maybe that's why he went back to his story. He wrote it during his first summer holidays as a teacher. He called it "The Fox Busters". 'When it was published I felt so proud!'

He felt grateful as well... to two special people. The first was Myrle who'd told him all along he could do it. The second was his publisher, Joanna Goldsworth. 'It was Joanna who helped me turn "The Fox Busters" into a good story,' Dick says. 'She taught me so much.'

DICK KING-SMITH

The Fox Busters

Puffin | Modern | Classics

Dick's first book

Dick's wife, Myrle

Before long, there were plenty more good stories by Dick King-Smith. One of them, "The Sheep Pig", won a special prize called The Guardian Award. It was the first of many.

A special shelf in Dick's study with some of the prizes that Dick's books have won.

Dick and Myrle dressed up to celebrate!

Two stars, Dick and Dodo, filming "Rub-A-Dub-Tub".

About this time, Dick met a television producer called Anne Wood. He appeared regularly on her children's TV series called "Rub-A-Dub-Tub" and "Pob". Dick was very famous after this. So was Dodo, his pet dachshund.

Soon he was writing about eight stories for children every year. Altogether, Dick is the author of more than a hundred books. He's sold more than five million copies worldwide.

How does he do it?

Each morning, Dick climbs the winding stairs of Diamond's Cottage.

A writer on his way to work...

His writing-room is tiny. It's full of books and pictures. Here, Dick writes on rough paper, using a pen. He stops after about two hours.

In the afternoon, he types out what he's written. His typewriter is very old - and he only uses one finger!

...and a writer at work.

Pages written, and typed, by Dick.

Is that all? Well, not quite.
    A writer never really stops working. Dick may be resting in his armchair or enjoying his garden. But who knows what he's thinking? 'Lots of ideas come whizzing into my mind,' he says. 'Most of

Dick with some framed artwork from his books

them are so batty I chuck them out again.' That's why, each evening he tests his stories on Myrle.
    Between them, they're usually right. So watch out for Dick's stories on television and as films at your local cinema. He's happiest writing books, though. Dick likes his stories best on the printed page.

Farmer Hogget and Babe... in the film based on Dick's classic "The Sheep Pig".

And I agree with him... don't you?

Important dates

1922	Dick King-Smith is born
1936-40	Goes to Marlborough College, Wiltshire
1941-46	War service in the Grenadier Guards
1943	Marries Myrle
1947-61	Runs farm for his father's company
1961	Father's company closes down
1961-67	Tenant farmer
1967-71	Dick works as a salesman, then in a shoe factory
1971-75	Trains to be a teacher at Bristol University
1975-82	Classteacher at Farmborough Primary School, Bath
1978	He publishes "The Fox Busters"
1982	Becomes a full-time writer
1984	"The Sheep Pig" wins The Guardian Award
1983-88	Dick appears regularly on television in "Rub-A-Dub-Tub" and "Pob"
1992	Voted Children's Author of the Year
1995	He wins the Children's Book Award
1996	The movie "Babe" is made from "The Sheep Pig"

Dick's garden even has a bronze statue of a pig!

Keywords

Guardian Award
A famous prize for children's books given by 'The Guardian' newspaper

magazine
Like a book, often with pictures, which is published regularly

publisher
Someone who organises the printing of a book

television producer
Someone who organises the making of a television programme

tenant farmer
A farmer who doesn't own the farm...but pays money to rent it

volunteer
Someone who offers help freely

Index